Gone West

Playwright

by

Baruch Menache

New York, NY

United States of America

Published by McWest & Associates

ISBN: 978-1-971928-46-3

Gone West is not written for conventional naturalist staging. It is composed as a poetic dramatic text, operating through verse, choral motion, and fractured monologue, rather than through linear plot progression or realistic dialogue exchange.

The work should be understood as a choral-driven verse drama. Individual characters; Rickle, Tory, the Owner, the Manager, the Chorus do not function solely as psychological individuals but as positions within a social and moral structure. Speech frequently exceeds character interiority and enters collective voice, historical echo, or ideological pressure. Repetition, fragmentation, and syntactic strain are deliberate and structural.

Dramatic action unfolds anti-naturalistically. Time is elastic, memory interrupts chronology, and scenes are organized by social conditions (labor, control, deprivation, rebellion) rather than by causal realism. The barracks, the field, the office, and the town are not locations in a realistic sense but zones of power and exposure.

The Chorus does not serve as commentary alone but as active social presence, articulating forces that individual characters cannot fully speak: economic pressure, moral judgment, inherited guilt, and communal complicity. At moments, individual characters enter choral speech; at others, the Chorus fractures into townsfolk, laborers, or observers. This fluidity is intentional.

Dramatis Personae

Rickle—a laborer; a speaking position within exhaustion and revolt

Tory—a laborer; a speaking position within memory and moral fracture

Older Man—a residual voice of instruction and inheritance

Owner—authority embodied; control without intimacy

Manager—administrative conscience and complicity

Captain—procedural force; law as repetition

Salamander—witness and interlocutor

Chorus—laborers, townsfolk, and collective voice

ACT: DAWN

[Pre-labor quiet; bodies already fatigued before work begins, Rickle's twitching suggests nervous energy rather than madness]

RICKLE

Roadster simpleton,

Friend or foe in the eyes

Tells he's Joe Journeyman

Making a buck or two with his back.

Twitching all over the place;

In some spirit he proclaims.

Never gonna get a full explanation;

A boy's little resilience of Lady Daphne,

Man's telling stance in the trenches,

Christmas peace of war-faring brothers.

TORY

Shan't brandy do the evil purge?

Namesake to the constitution folk,

Them learned bearers, Franklin's men.

Ain't sunshine gonna slip on by,

Fellows on by the mud swamp

Digging their way to gold.

Fortune as scripture promised,

Sanctioned by sworn preacher men.

OLDER MAN

Sat through Bilbe class, heard less than a word

Gonna be front-line torch bearing on a crusade.

March to the top real fast,

That'll be the kid that never spells

But get them holy words carved on skin.

RICKLE

Wildflower lost its princess,

As' be good as the next feller

Does the honest waging go.

He's know all there's to know,

'Bout the good life in all.

Bounce the lone soldier

Reaping from a weak crop;

Lonely is his name tag,

Sifting flour and dirty sheets.

Tried his lot, many to's misfortune,

Chilled a barrel for a go at lightning.

Says the Lord gonna hold back for them simple folk.

Says the Lord gonna hold back for them simple folk.

TORY

Features as good as talk, grace minded by the lot of men.

Sayin' words in filling gaps, thinking fables age;

Them grace moves the cow right over the hill.

RICKLE

Youth made of myth, darings of cattle courage;

Hero's mess, momma's scattered fascinations;

Researcher's tabloid, city folk scare.

Going towards the heat grinder,

Be it murder—a capital joy

As when wanted folk meet capital demise.

Cried yearlong worries for evil purged

Makes towns' name an afterthought.

TORY

Fear is to know yonder the average man,

Hail the man who's known the street,

Asphalt, concrete and wood decor;

For cradle, care and home core.

ACT: THE FIELD

TORY

> Fanciful spoons of daytime merriment,
>
> Lonesome here in traditional bowels.
>
> Preached to the unlivin' choir
>
> Singing praises to timber weeds.

RICKLE

> Raisin' grain aback the shoulder strap,
>
> Hopeful rain don't come so soon,
>
> Yearning educated man's glimmer.
>
> Downtown a'cross that bar
>
> Wives and youthful kids
>
> Blushing a strangers' smile.
>
> Do the American way,
>
> Strollers' side-by-side coal.

Tellin' souls their determination,
Hasn't destiny retraced the tree?
Riots raisin' banners of plastic color,
Devising hearts waved to glare.

[Owner shows up]

Owner

>Men at Work! Move to your hole;
>
>If there ain't, dig rather deep,
>
>Dirt that cannot be cleansed;
>
>Mark the working tattoo!

[To himself]

Tory

>Years solace to the backpacker
>
>Skipping a solstice or two,
>
>Knows not his name nor occupation
>
>Yet makes steps his dissertation,
>
>Boulders and street lamps his thesis.

[As owner leaves]

Owner

>Harley knew none of y'all
>
>Shaking boots on mudded ground
>
>Frolicking the neighbor's pass-way
>
>As though he, king of the free world.

[Owner leaves]

Rickle

>Made a friend in the outback

Liquored rooms of rebel folk

Promises over dreams;

Scrawny dreams to tell ya,

Pasted by goings and comings.

TORY

Bellowed by unassuming windstorms

A jokester has given a laugh,

Shaking all over for the jibe.

Is grand! 'Tis life, smocked of all failings.

Tricked of meaning, thee generation merriest

Upon rocks and silhouettes of inconsequence,

To prove immortality and uproot mine own.

Ha! You laugh for offering existence

If mediocrity or showmanship proved worth.

RICKLE

In the rebellion of bespoken attempt,

Tinkling the scar right over the skin.

Made by distraction or another rebellion.

To measure revolutionary spirit,

To mark a name in sand,

Wash'd from a shore.

Rebel! Be my rebellion, stand!

TORY

To prove that you can stand,

Fight to prove otherwise.

Time stretched through space.

ACT: THE PLAN

[They begin to plan the rebellion]

RICKLE

> After lunch will be my moment,
>
> 'Till that dinner poach;
>
> On my way home
>
> When that glow do no reach.

TORY

> With a heart promising
>
> Another day of revenge,
>
> From the spirit of today
>
> Tasking yesterday.

RICKLE

> I know the grim-face is coming
>
> Yet nothing to do.
>
> Cheer will not repose
>
> Nor the hemlock dish.

Wishing to retain a loss

As we enter oblivion

Of a winter harvest.

TORY

It shows itself

In the rubble of dysphoria.

What goes there

Does not return.

To the everglading show,

Glowing right over the creak.

[Late at night to himself]

TORY

A warm heart under guise of disruption,

Under the welling spring,

Delighted and uninterrupted.

Choice'd pieces, troubling displeasure,

For I am no God, no creator, no creation.

Barr me, six miles to count.

Do not allow me entrance—

A glance, a glimpse, a sight.

Engaging the prowl enemy with sticks
Bearers of swords mended thought to action,
Yonder of predatory instinct and bare hands
Gave way to motion and quicken spirit.

She sits with promise,
Revel of a different world.
She holds a future in soft hands
That will not participate in this skirmish.

ACT: DAY TWO

[Next morning]

TORY

Reckless and centered,

Trident and succulent.

What about this life?—

Tis go from afar to close

'nd merry when none is sought.

When withering becomes a delight

As fear grips the night;

Noon-fairy is 'round the clock

Tickling the last dog's growl.

RICKLE

Simple made and triple wade,

Spelled 'n grave, simple yet spade.

A system of weeds

Chore'd and sampled.

Whence wishes are granted,

For grace gives duty.

Knot tied its stubborn way;

Warp wont the dignity worth,

Chosen as a matter of choice;

Trailing crumbs after deserts.

Tory

Dawn exposed, nightingales halt;

Beauty skims its fat in a crowd.

Witness assesses to tell in kind;

Ain't that a wonder, ain't rewarded in twos!

Trust be more virtue than vice,

For in the fall lives a sense.

Vice backs the corner room

Where defeat exposed sorrow,

Alls' left to mark the destruction.

Rickle

Weakened mind and satiated heart

They did a number on me,

Unseen by the morning sun.

Witnesses scattered, latency delivered.

Bewildered to the sideline,

Delivery forgets the address,

Distribution from a center

Which no longer brights with life.

[Friend, noticing discomfort]

SALAMANDER

Are you the man—

Who goes borrowing through entranceways—

Of doorways undisclosed?

Shading halfway glances,

Ashamed but unaware?

Or, are you the man—

Who sits under a microscopic glance

To the tearful drops,

Of a work-full duty?

Are you such a man?

Tedious is his job,

Recognizing the angles

Of hurtful foe,

Of dangerous proponents, of ridicule.

If you are such a man,

Then meet us too—

These two men,

On equal footing,

To make it through.

RICKLE

Repetition muttering like a pond to evening grace.

Don't you see my rebellion? My revolution?

As the river-girls showed the way;

Truest in mascara, eye shadow licked.

TORY

Hearts won't be mended

Before war marks territory.

Try me at midnight, I'll admit another way.

RICKLE

Joyous in rebellion,

Gracious to the info-lot

Teethed to the facilitator,

To cherish the unsuspecting.

Bridge moments of ecstasy,

Sample the excess of void lost.

Is this the occasion that makes for a leap?

ACT: MORNING THREE

[Morning]

[Owner entering barracks, barracks no longer feel neutral; they are controlled space]

OWNER

> You shake boots on firm ground,
>
> Don't ya?
>
> All coddled after a layer or two of warmth?
>
> Deserter ya 're not
>
> Full of morning's cold air,
>
> 'Stablish somethin' for my rules.
>
> Mister be ready to leave,
>
> Air's been staled of lazy,
>
> Off you go to a gray horizon,
>
> Departing a promising embrace.

[At work]

TORY

> Sitting on a pile,

High indeed,

Of wishes and promises—

Told to sleep.

Now banished from my refuge,

For the oath taken by mine wings.

T 'were we must fly to rid of you

And dread of loss naught to remain.

[Working]

RICKLE

Geared in position,

Rickety to the tee,

Trickity to the three,

In count and in motion.

Screws and bolts to ones and zeros,

Arms and banter for code and source,

Day's earned work to nighttime chill.

Better or worse was never the question.

To give man reason to live,

Before tanket—tookatoo

Finds no refuge in the one-to-two.

SALAMANDER

Slowly makes in the outback,

Ideal as to be expected.

Ruffling Earth's brow,

Painstaking as always.

Wind over the lost gander,

Lamp all lacquered in yellow.

To carry what cannot be fulfilled

To linger what will be lost

To stay the wretched path

To endure a repetition

To settle a lost dream.

TORY

Renowned in the age of innocence

Which can no longer afford

This sentimental value.

The overflow must have done him in.

They remembered his dreams,

Fantasies at the wayside.

Overrun; the cause of default.

RICKLE

> To pledge allegiance,
> Rotary gears in motionless state
> Mechanized for the grunt.
>
> Sighed a'way the wind,
> Melancholy, as I wish.
> Jitters for excitement,
> Dare tell Mary in support of my freedom.
>
> Brushing those fields of some gesture,
> Love, is it that Tory?
>
> If I find myself merry
> To more than movements
> Or find tranquil in a storage room.
> When seventeen was just a number,
> Placated against my insecure wall.

TORY

> Marked by time
> What a thing!

Must we watch the demise,
Shelter to witness the stance
Of a grieved reluctance.

Saying grace goes with beauty
Knows nothing of misfortune,
Wanting the best of form.

Dignity's last spark
As embers find way to dust,
Calmly laying ash,
Light as a feather;
Mark of consumption.

RICKLE

Dare you not—gray!
That color of pronouncement.
Haven't enough to show yourself
Under the nightly sun?
Without regret of a noble face.

Are you not more bleak than black?
Where it knows its place

Behind white love and sweet dove.

Hadn't you the spirit of leathered red?

That enjoyed a sacrifice?

Be gone, gray!

With callousness and disfavor

The deception of it all!

You consumed more than fire

Tricked more than a white rose

Stolen heart from someone who loved

Taken cradle of no return in sight.

You gray monster, satisfied with the claim

Haven't you the decency to regard the
consumption?

Or attempt a change?

Oblivion is your choice,

To take all that's around you,

Until my love becomes true,

And gray is forgotten forever.

ACT: THE SECRET

[In the owner's office]

OWNER

> They came on by train tracks,
>
> Down by hollow creek,
>
> Blackened by coal.

MANAGER

> They know not your neighbor nor friend,
>
> Their smile, for charcoaled teeth in blanked state.
>
> Is anyone going to give them existence?

OWNER

> They stand for our sitting
>
> Make way when day should end,
>
> Find favor to bring loss
>
> And always depart a shining sun.

[Owner leaves, Rickle enters]

MANAGER

> You see the spirit
>
> Has gained the upper hand.
>
> Nothing to do
>
> But be a man wished for.

RICKLE

> I trust you will keep a secret
>
> That cannot reach public ears.
>
> The gist I will tell
>
> If you promise secrecy.
>
> Alas, I will pronounce the hidden.

MANAGER

> Freed the cold daybreak
>
> Ghastly rival-spirit buckles in
>
> Making wild claims on desert sands.
>
> Seems awfully nice,
>
> A cool breeze 'fore sundown.

RICKLE

Breaching an ocean pile of stardust!

Yellin 'nto windstorms,

Hiding of shielded remorse.

Sand as rivers in palace gardens

Ghosted into weatherly paths,

Sun quenched of spring delight.

Daybreak offers rest upon rest;

Nightfall for infallibility,

Twilight chills existence.

Do you take me as I am?

All reckless and kind?

ACT: TORY'S CHILDHOOD

TORY'S MOTHER

> Spoken in that gentlemanly way,
>
> Fumbled words engraved in stone.
>
> Shoe maker's daring dream;
>
> Scrubby toes to dinner wine.

TORY'S FATHER

> Wives hold on back for joyous retreats
>
> Of rich mongers and tales of fortune.
>
> Received the mustache grin that'll get ya booked,
>
> Old wagers nearsighted of great company,
>
> Shows a man's worth in charismatic fondness.

[He leaves]

TORY'S MOTHER

> The one time he met JFK in Nevada plains

Reveling the meager man's slice of bread,

Though mysterious in blackened coal,

Attaching the wagon in a heavy snowfall;

Sweet to smirk the platitude from plenitude,

Plans from a damp office in conquest of illusion,

Shelter from bread and oats, barley or milk,

Take rather an extra chandelier and no bulbs.

[Sighing from her husband and state]
Swarms of beans and lentil plush,

Cracked leatherback memorabilia,

Second-hand smiles and third-hand jokes.

TORY'S MOTHERS' FRIEND

Tobacca' and coffee mixed in jest.

He's merry with child's eye

Whose glimmer is suspect?

Of dad's rebellion to the global spin.

The isolated rich dreaming of poorness,

Licking vanilla with no promise of dinner.

Fatherly grim of a better life,

Calloused hands offer with no reserve.

Promised sandy dreams;

The smile, alive, the grin full.

[He pops back in]

TORY'S FATHER

Driving a mule steering hilly curves;

Horses travel alongside the breeze.

Swaddling through mud-paths

Loading weighty rocks.

TORY'S MOTHERS' FRIEND

Daringly enough to move spirits

Awakened lioness from a caged slumber

Sadness awaits this afternoon repast

Moaning as for tactical advantage;

Wires, ropes and the tourists' smile.

TORY'S MOTHER

To love thy kind

Known behest from a jest,

Stutter the grace of a king

Holden seat higher than man.

ACT: CONFUSION

[Sunday in the barracks]

[Tension is high, Sunday removes work but not control]

TORY

To relieve tension,

To find success

In the self-made man.

Proclaimed maker and made;

Responsible and responsive;

Lover and loved.

RICKLE

A twinkling sensation,

What goes the sailor's intuition—

County and Sheriff

Make mockery of me,

Squired to deny airy daylight,

Surpassing this denial of parts.

Alas, he did tell of something,

Get the mailer back!

I speak right to their eyes

And without hesitation I say,

"I am citizen."

So hurry off and bring my silk napkin

So I can continue to enrich the king.

Then I will find the majority and be its minority,

For they must be on the lookout for a citizen.

SALAMANDER

How goes the spark of one's name?

Drags along in high school,

Finds merit in an office space,

Bolsters confidence in a fatherly way.

RICKLE

If we were to take a boat,

I would wonder about a plane.

SALAMANDER

Stationed at work,

Worker of the land.

Country boy he's told to be,

Or else stamp that flag's honor

As be preacher in high noon,

Awhile townsfolk sip nightly liquid.

ACT: THE ARREST

[Arrest is procedural, not dramatic]

MANAGER

[To himself]

My compassion for thee
Has overlooked thy or thee,
Unless—bearing unlimited supply
To which my frail humanness be gone;
I will love all of thy being indifferent to love.

Sameness kindles the fading flame
Likeness dost shame love bearings,
Unity repulsive to the grand stranger,
Reckon workers' plight to feeble ground,
Unionized at peril of any wage.
Burning a-thousand cathedrals to utter despair,
Grant saints' glimpse to burn one's savior
And foreskin contested to burn bridges.

[Enter Rickle]

MANAGER

> You must come here,
> Delightful treats
> Of merry cheer,
> Daytime dreams
> Of future promises.
>
> Can't we attribute mistakes to prolonging?
> Those meant to wither away?
> To make immortal
> What was destined no more.
>
> The longing for what was
> In what is.
> To be as it were
> Where 's I belong to me.
> The burden of present
> Owed to all
> And none to me.

RICKLE

> Sayin' ripples of tricks

To damn a softened heart.

Fears the long run in an instant,

Catcher to shaky boots in a mud-pile.

Dost know a thing 'bout despair?

Time is its fortress with words of vain.

Backed to a corner sees no walls;

Homage loses stride to withered grass.

Sorry to see the glad man, all glad in all.

[Enter captain, they arrest Tory and Rickle]

CAPTAIN

Owner man has the ear of the captain,

He's paid dues of civil stock,

Made a man outta' these boots

With bearings of praise,

Granting the wife's skip,

Shoulders the gold in my badge,

No fills a gun barrel with drudges.

Hearsay is your existence,

Stakes without window shutters.

Who's the citizen of the road?

Can't speak from a plot of land!

TORY

Said never the ocean of land folk

Tsunami takes breath of cotton and corn,

Goes the street to offer any smarts,

To bed is the officer and meager land,

Church to state gives civil to none

'Ought say the Spanish.

Fatten a stomach that is not your own,

Close the streets to make barren the crop;

Your moment in history is our yellow backs.

Three generations has the rebellious son

Overlook the stench of fool

That'll make love with grass.

ACT: THE SISTER

[Six years prior]

[Tory's sister walks past town, retrospective indictment of social morality]

ONE TOWNSFOLK

Double-bind sets choice's fallacy;

Towns square vocalizes barren woman,

Aged men frolics the adages of her own,

Kisses a conscience or constitutional oath.

ANOTHER TOWNSFOLK

She'd make rolls outta fine flour

Smocked of that dirty apron,

Sold crisp for unmarried years,

Sat to the tune of millionaires' row.

ONE TOWNSFOLK

Sought man in the hands of man

Dared enough naked and soft,

The lion, king; the bear, queen.

To crown a beast for flesh and blood

Despisin' the family god in utter disgust.

[She is tattered and unkempt]

ANOTHER TOWNSFOLK

Winner is the feat of a slumbered man,

Awakened to demised features,

As be better if never contested

Than be contested and fall to knees.

Bucklin' to a Joe or 'a Fiona

Who's made credence of destitute.

Can't blame them though,

Joe-Fiona to be married.

Love breaks all, doesn't it?

Feels burden in lost sleep.

Yes, sir, for love you say, and love we do.

SISTER

Filing nails to cover evermore cracks,

Slippin' an apron to robe a wife,

Thought the female barge was left in school,

Softer with naked legs to share the next crop.

They's tell a lady lover that sits in sand,

Reads Jane Austen to her romance,

Husband of a sure type of husbandry

Likened for smooth nails,

Or afternoon for its namesake.

RICKLE

Reaching for a prayer in exile terms

Is fillin' oil to a used lamp wick;

A reminder of detested depths.

Tears cheaper than water,

Embracing the neighboring mammal.

Silver lake dost winters' quiet mark

Reveled soundscape of broken grounds.

Dig deep they say, dig rather deep.

Choice-making sits to the tune of West,
Chasing the empire of deeds misplaced.
Seconding the evermore resolution
That jitters the cotton plantation.

Sincere to a job-making stance
Workin' the pike stick that'll testify,
Existence of the job-man all stretched
To the mighty pike stick that'll testify.

The crop mongers, dishing produce in soil grain,
Bushels to the ton, workers in the yen.
Wreaking overlords tellin' 'em how to be,
Chasin' squirrels that eat the vegetable patch,
Six months from the last harvest;
Tells' it's the suit man who don't care.

Chills the youngster's tamed yearning
Seeking resolute a 'liken' Uncle Mike,
Serves higher than the minimum
Offering no maximum an award.
Finds grace in the dollar or its double.

Dust blows the underpass gathering,
Selling a story of something or another.
Should see his eyes in determination,
It'll show strength of a missed mark.
Famed the insolence of the over-coached,
Namesake apt attention with credulity.